KEN STABLER, MARCUS ALLEN, PETE BANASZAK, FRED BILETNIKOFF, TIM BROWN, DAVE CASPER, ART SHELL, LINCOLN KENNEDY, GENE UPSHAW, STEVE WISNIEWSKI, JIM OTTO, HOWIE LONG, BEN DAVIDSON, OTIS SISTRUNK, CHESTER MCGLOCKTON, ROD MARTIN, MATT MILLEN, TED HENDRICKS, WILLIE BROWN, MIKE HAYNES, JACK TATUM, GEORGE ATKINSON, GEORGE BLANDA, RAY GUY, KEN STABLER, MARCUS ALLEN, PETE BANASZAK, FRED BILETNIKOFF, TIM BROWN, DAVE CASPER, ART SHELL, LINCOLN KENNEDY, GENE UPSHAW, STEVE WISNIEWSKI

THE STORY OF THE RAIDERS

RAIDERS
4
RAIDERS

THE STORY OF THE RAIDERS

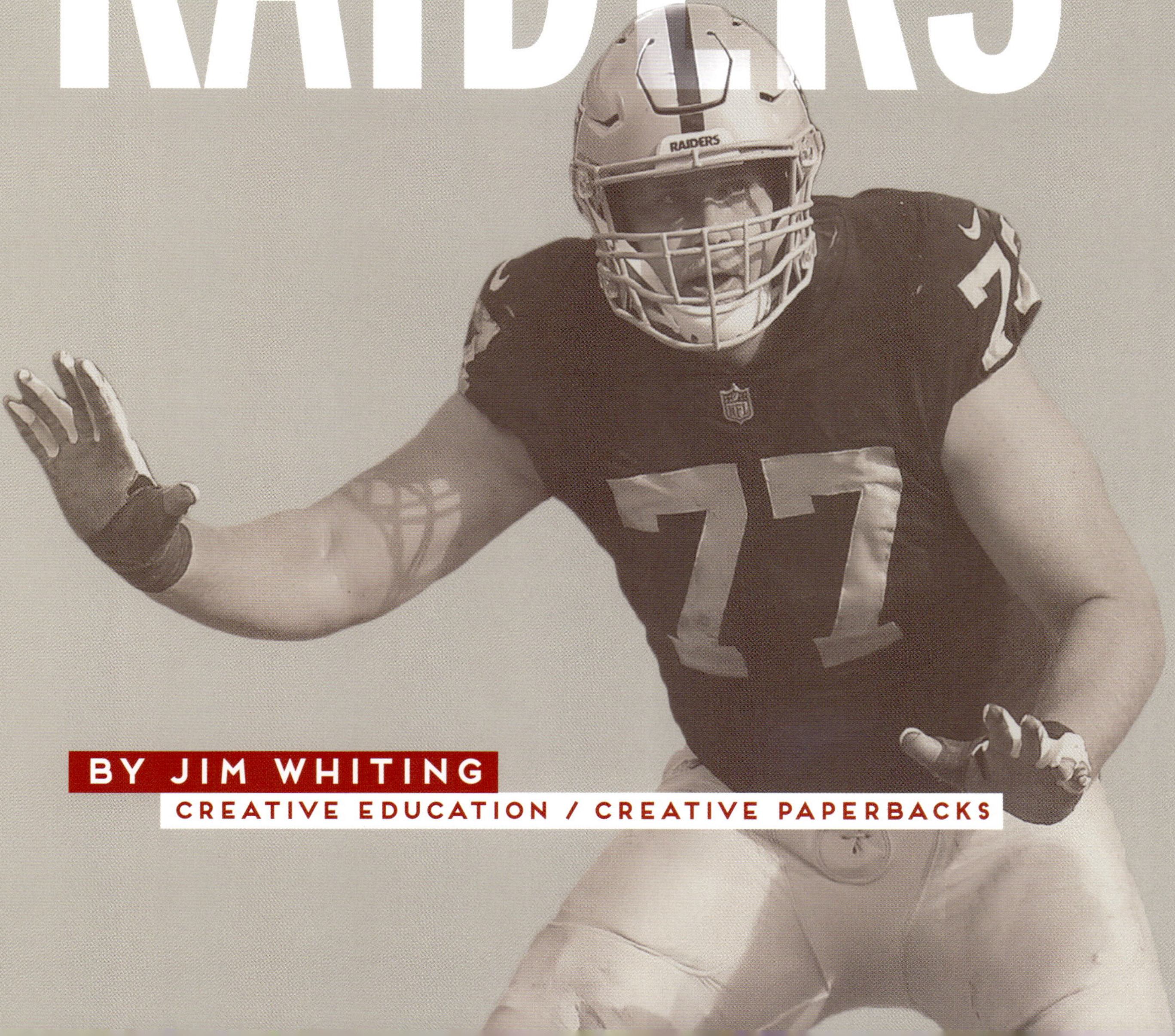

BY JIM WHITING

CREATIVE EDUCATION / CREATIVE PAPERBACKS

PUBLISHED BY CREATIVE EDUCATION AND CREATIVE PAPERBACKS
P.O. BOX 227, MANKATO, MINNESOTA 56002
CREATIVE EDUCATION AND CREATIVE PAPERBACKS ARE IMPRINTS OF THE CREATIVE COMPANY
WWW.THECREATIVECOMPANY.US

DESIGN AND PRODUCTION BY BLUE DESIGN (WWW.BLUEDES.COM)
ART DIRECTION BY RITA MARSHALL
PRINTED IN CHINA

PHOTOGRAPHS BY AP IMAGES (ASSOCIATED PRESS), CORBIS (BETTMANN), GETTY IMAGES (BERNSTEIN ASSOCIATES, BETTMANN, ROB BROWN, KEVIN C. COX, STEPHEN DUNN, DAVID EULITT, JAMES FLORES/NFL PHOTOS, FOCUS ON SPORT, GRANT HALVERSON, THEARON W. HENDERSON, GEORGE LONG/NFL, JOHN G. MABANGLO/AFP, TAKASHI MAKITA/NFL, AL MESSERSCHMIDT/NFL, RONALD C. MODRA/SPORTS IMAGERY, NFL, MIKE POWELL, PRO FOOTBALL HALL OF FAME/NFL PHOTOS, EZRA SHAW, JAMIE SQUIRE, GREG TROTT, MICHAEL ZAGARIS)

NAMES: WHITING, JIM, AUTHOR.
TITLE: THE STORY OF THE RAIDERS / JIM WHITING.
SERIES: NFL TODAY.
INCLUDES INDEX.
SUMMARY: THIS HIGH-INTEREST HISTORY OF THE NATIONAL FOOTBALL LEAGUE'S RAIDERS HIGHLIGHTS MEMORABLE GAMES, SUMMARIZES SEASONAL TRIUMPHS AND DEFEATS, AND FEATURES STANDOUT PLAYERS SUCH AS TIM BROWN.
IDENTIFIERS: LCCN 2018059139 / ISBN 978-1-64026-154-9 (HARDCOVER) / ISBN 978-1-62832-717-5 (PBK) / ISBN 978-1-64000-272-2 (EBOOK)
SUBJECTS: LCSH: OAKLAND RAIDERS (FOOTBALL TEAM)—HISTORY—JUVENILE LITERATURE. / LOS ANGELES RAIDERS (FOOTBALL TEAM)—HISTORY—JUVENILE LITERATURE.
CLASSIFICATION: LCC GV956.024 W55 2019 / DDC 796.33209794/66—DC23

FIRST EDITION HC 9 8 7 6 5 4 3 2 1
FIRST EDITION PBK 9 8 7 6 5 4 3 2 1

COVER: KOLTON MILLER
PAGE 2: DEREK CARR
PAGES 6–7: JAMARCUS RUSSELL

RAIDERS
75
GU

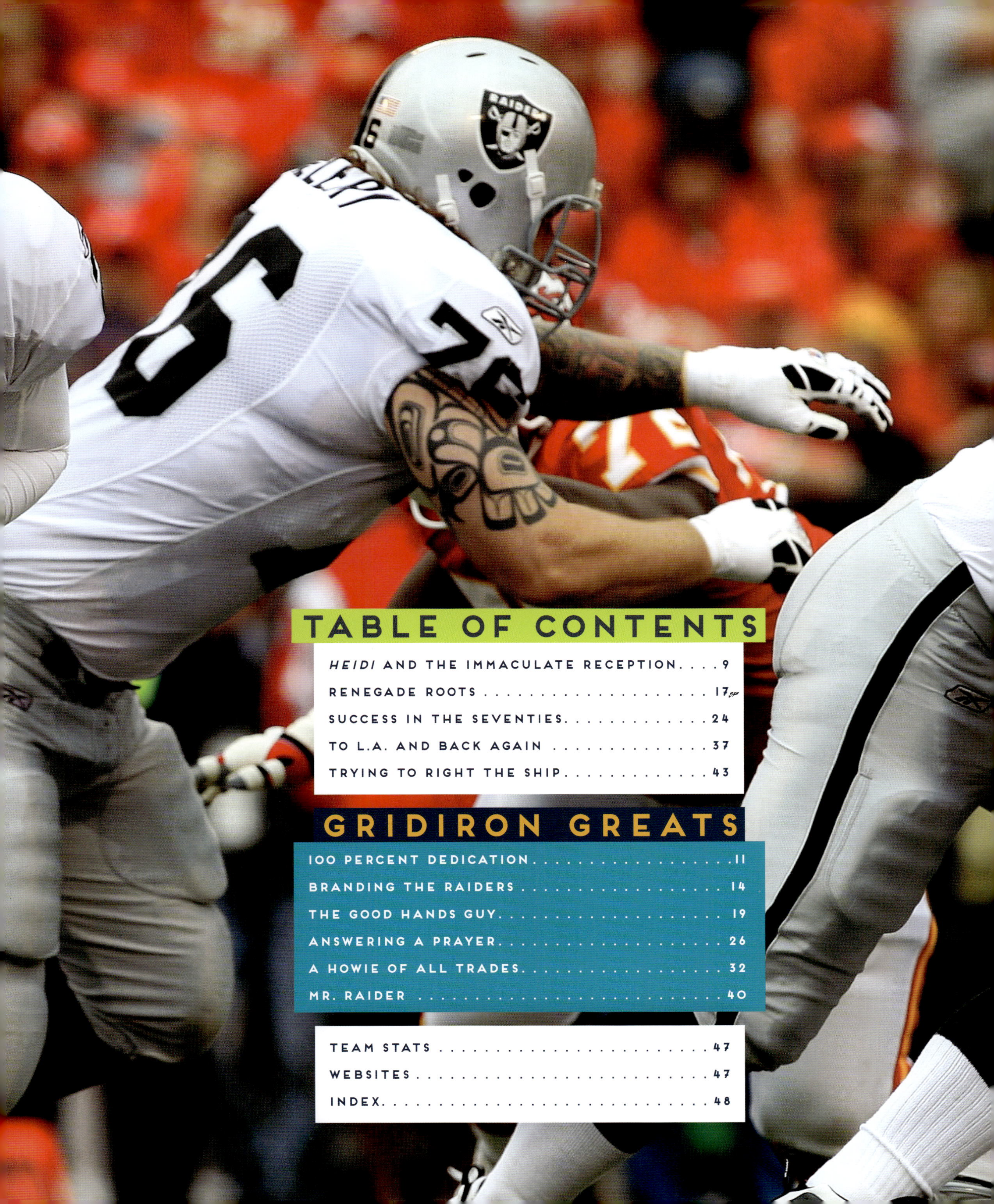

TABLE OF CONTENTS

GRIDIRON GREATS

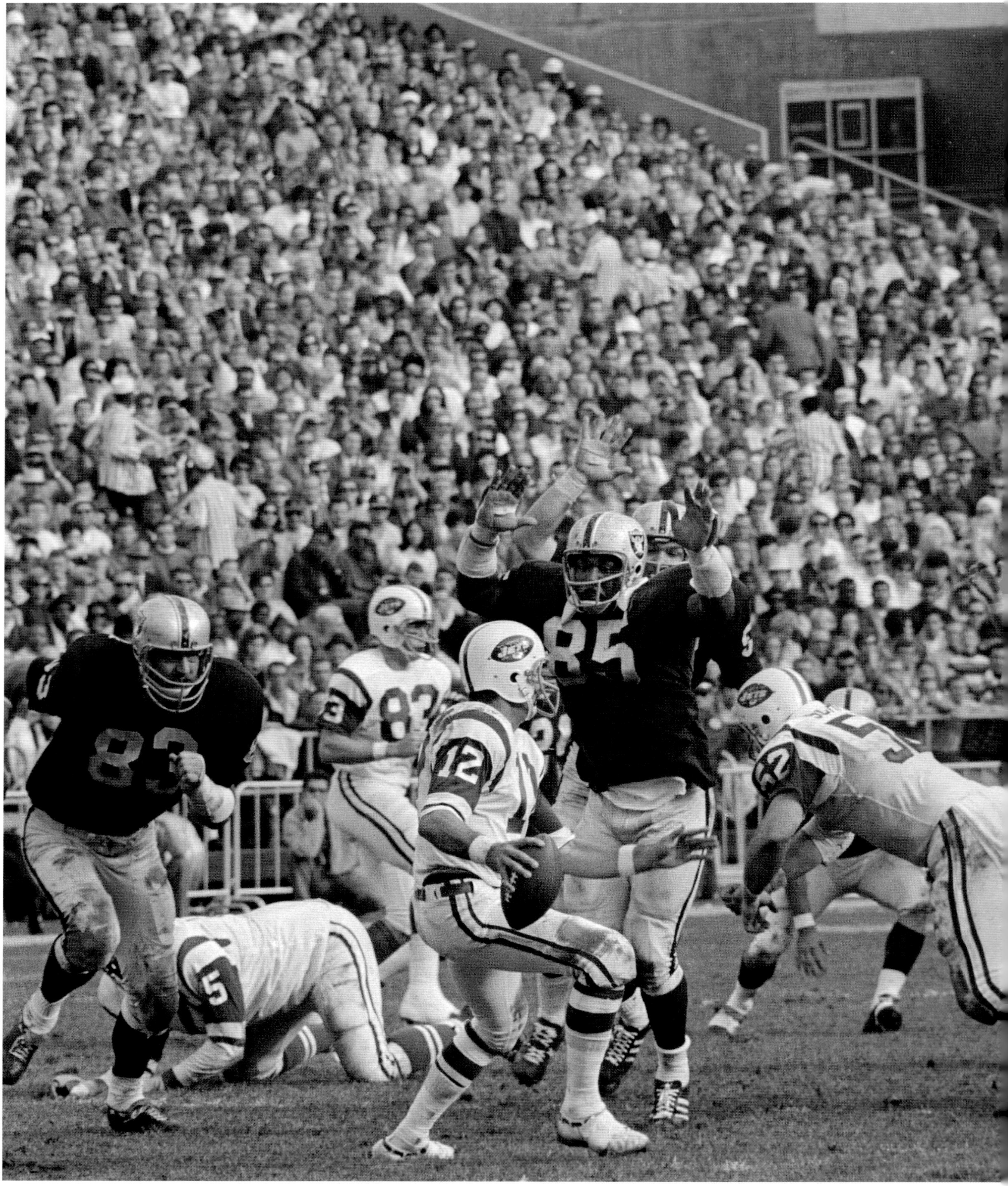

DEFENSIVE TACKLE CARLETON OATS (NUMBER 85)

HEIDI AND THE IMMACULATE RECEPTION

Some National Football League (NFL) games are so famous that they have nicknames. The "Ice Bowl." The "Monday Night Miracle." The "Greatest Game Ever Played." The "Sneakers Game." Memorable plays have also received nicknames. "The Catch." The "Music City Miracle." "Elway's Helicopter Ride." According to some, the Oakland Raiders rank number one in both categories.

On November 17, 1968, Oakland hosted the New York Jets. There were eight lead changes or ties. The Jets finally seemed to have the game under control. With just over a minute left, they took a 32–29 lead. But the Raiders came back with a quick touchdown. Then, the Jets fumbled the kickoff. Oakland running back Preston Ridlehuber scooped up the loose ball. He barreled into the end zone. Oakland won, 43–32.

Fans buzzed about the outcome. But not because of the game itself. The NBC television network was scheduled to start the movie *Heidi* at 7 P.M. When the Jets scored their last field goal, NBC executives assumed the game was over. They switched to *Heidi* everywhere except on the West Coast. Fans were outraged that they had missed the exciting finish. The network was bombarded by complaints. Later, NBC issued a public apology. "Probably the most significant factor to come out of *Heidi* was, whatever you do, you better not leave an NFL football game," said Val Pinchbeck, the NFL's former chief of broadcasting. In 1997, a media group voted the "Heidi Game" as the league's most memorable regular-season matchup.

Many fans think the greatest play in NFL history happened during a playoff game between Oakland and the Pittsburgh Steelers. It was December 23, 1972. The Raiders led, 7–6. Just 22 seconds remained. Steelers quarterback Terry Bradshaw hurled the ball downfield. Pittsburgh running back John Fuqua leaped for the catch. So did Raiders safety Jack Tatum. The ball was deflected. It popped into the air. Steelers running back Franco Harris was trailing the play. He snagged the ball inches off the turf and lumbered into the end zone.

LEFT: HEIDI AND HER GRANDFATHER

GRIDIRON GREATS

100 PERCENT DEDICATION

Al Davis never played professional football. Yet he took over as head coach of the Raiders in 1963. He became the living symbol of the team. His wardrobe consisted mostly of black, white, and silver warm-up suits. Later, Davis often wore a Super Bowl ring on each hand. He sported dark sunglasses and a slicked-back hairstyle. "His life is the Raiders," explained former special teams coach Steve Ortmayer. "He has never taken a day off from the Raiders. Never." Through the years, Davis served in six different positions. These included player personnel assistant, assistant coach, head coach, general manager, league commissioner, and principal owner.

AL DAVIS
HEAD COACH, TEAM OWNER

RAIDERS SEASONS:
1963–65 (AS HEAD COACH),
1966–2011 (AS OWNER)

JACK TATUM

RAIDERS FANS HAVE GIVEN THE "IMMACULATE RECEPTION" A DIFFERENT NAME: "IMMACULATE DECEPTION."

The score sparked an immediate controversy. At that time, if a pass touched an offensive player first, he was the only one who could catch the ball. But if a defensive player made the first contact, any offensive player could catch it. The same was true if both players touched it at the same time. No official had a clear view of the play. Still, they declared that it was a touchdown. Pittsburgh won. "It remains the most incredible, implausible finish of a football game," Oakland center Jim Otto later said. The play became known as the "Immaculate Reception." Raiders fans have given it a different name: "Immaculate Deception." They claim "the public was deceived, the officials were deceived, and we were deceived."

GRIDIRON GREATS
BRANDING THE RAIDERS

Early on, the Raiders had trouble getting off the ground. Then Al Davis took over. His first order of business was to develop the team's image. He started with the logo. He created a shield with crossed swords. Over it, a "raider," or pirate, wore an old-time football helmet. Davis also trademarked his team's slogans, such as "Just Win, Baby." Davis knew none of these changes would work without on-field success. Soon, the Raiders had that, too. They became a powerhouse in the 1970s. "What's important is winning," Davis said. "In my culture, in our culture, in the Raider Culture."

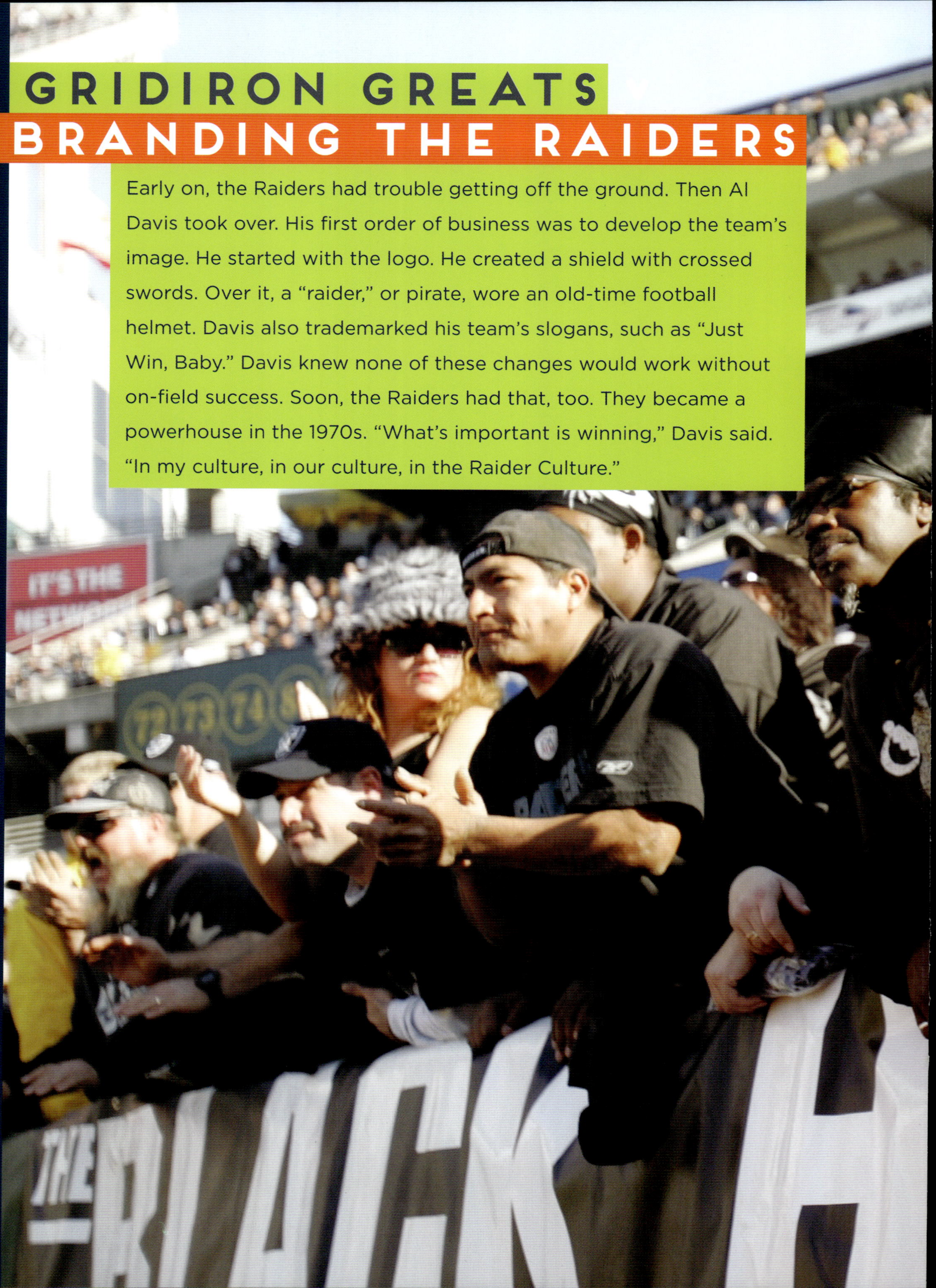

RAIDERS

RAIDERS VS. DALLAS TEXANS, 1960

RENEGADE ROOTS

Before 1960, Oakland did not have a major professional sports team. In 1960, the American Football League (AFL) was created to compete with the NFL. Oakland was the last team to be added. Team officials chose Raiders as the nickname. At first, it referred to pirates. It soon was used to describe outlaws in general.

The Raiders struggled in their first season. They wore used uniforms that a college had sold them. Despite being based in Oakland, their home field was not in the city. They

76

76 CAREER TOUCHDOWNS

190

190 GAMES PLAYED

FRED BILETNIKOFF
WIDE RECEIVER

RAIDERS SEASONS: 1965–78
HEIGHT: 6-FOOT-1
WEIGHT: 190 POUNDS

GRIDIRON GREATS
THE GOOD HANDS GUY

Fred Biletnikoff never dazzled anyone with his speed. Instead, he was a tough, hard-nosed, go-to receiver. He was not afraid of running across the middle of the field where linebackers might crush him. With superb hand-eye coordination, he could catch even the worst passes. “The guy can catch anything he can touch,” coach John Madden said. “That’s no accident. Some receivers might catch 15 passes in practice. Fred will stick around and catch 100.” He entered the Pro Football Hall of Fame in 1988. Today, the annual Biletnikoff Award honors the best receiver in college football.

JIM OTTO

GENE UPSHAW

shared Kezar Stadium in San Francisco with the NFL's 49ers. The Raiders scrounged for talent. They found some in quarterback Tom Flores and center Jim Otto. Many fans remember Otto's "00" jersey number. It matched the first and last letters of his name. "I could make some NFL clubs, I know," Otto said. "But it's more of an honor and distinction to be an original member of a brand-new league." The young Raiders started slowly. They only won nine games during their first three years.

Things improved in 1963. Al Davis took over as coach and general manager. He began to build an intimidating team image. He outfitted his players in silver-and-black uniforms. The Raiders jumped to 10–4 that season. Davis was the AFL's Coach of the Year. In 1966, he briefly served as AFL commissioner. Later that year, he returned to Oakland as general manager and part-owner. By then, the team had several talented players. Wide receiver Fred Biletnikoff grabbed passes from quarterback Daryle "Mad Bomber" Lamonica. Guard Gene Upshaw anchored the offensive line.

Lamonica threw 30 touchdown passes in 1967. Oakland surged to 13–1. It beat the Houston Oilers in the AFL Championship Game. The Raiders marched to Super Bowl II. Legendary coach Vince Lombardi and his NFL champion Green Bay Packers beat them, 33–14. The

"I COULD MAKE SOME NFL CLUBS, I KNOW. BUT IT'S MORE OF AN HONOR AND DISTINCTION TO BE AN ORIGINAL MEMBER OF A BRAND-NEW LEAGUE."

—JIM OTTO

Raiders had served notice, though. They were a force to be reckoned with.

John Madden became head coach in 1969. The Raiders went 12–1–1. They stomped the Oilers, 56–7, in the playoffs. But the Kansas City Chiefs ousted them in the next round. The AFL and the NFL merged in 1970. Oakland topped the American Football Conference (AFC) West Division. It faced the Baltimore Colts in the conference championship game. The Colts prevailed, 27–17. The Raiders missed the 1971 playoffs. They improved to 10–3–1 in 1972. But the Steelers beat them in the playoffs with the "Immaculate Reception."

JOHN MADDEN AND
DARYLE LAMONICA

SUCCESS IN THE SEVENTIES

KEN STABLER

Ken Stabler became the regular starting quarterback in 1973. The Raiders remained strong through the 1970s. The team became known for its fearsome defense. Tatum was nicknamed "The Assassin." He was a fierce tackler. Ted Hendricks was a versatile, 6-foot-7 linebacker. He was known as "The Mad Stork." Cornerback Willie Brown did not need a nickname. He grabbed 39 interceptions during his Raiders career. The Raiders reached the conference championship game in 1973, 1974, and 1975. Unfortunately, they lost every time. Oakland soon developed a reputation as a team that could not win the big one.

WEEK 2

RAIDERS VS. SAN DIEGO CHARGERS

SAN DIEGO, CALIFORNIA
SEPTEMBER 10, 1978

GRIDIRON GREATS

ANSWERING A PRAYER

The “Holy Roller” is a famous Oakland play. It occurred on the last play of a 1978 game. The Raiders trailed the San Diego Chargers, 20–14. They had the ball on the Chargers’ 14-yard line. Quarterback Ken Stabler was being tackled. He intentionally fumbled the ball forward. Running back Pete Banaszak batted the ball toward the goal line. Tight end Dave Casper (pictured) awkwardly fell on it in the end zone. The score tied the game. Errol Mann’s extra point kick sealed the win. “It would’ve been nicer to do it a little smoother,” Casper joked, “with a little more skill and like a dancer or something.”

84

84 RUSHING YARDS (OAKLAND)

197

197 RUSHING YARDS (SAN DIEGO)

KEN STABLER

In 1976, Stabler tossed 27 touchdown passes. The defense was stronger than ever. Oakland finished 13–1. The Raiders squeezed by the New England Patriots in the first round of the playoffs. They demolished Pittsburgh to win the AFC Championship Game. Then, they faced the Minnesota Vikings in Super Bowl XI. Upshaw and tackle Art Shell gave the Raiders a strong offensive line. They blew open holes for fullback Mark van Eeghen and running back Clarence Davis. The Raiders compiled 266 rushing yards. They beat the Vikings, 32–14. It was their first Super Bowl title.

The Raiders came back strong in 1977. They went 11–3. In the first round of the playoffs, they faced the Colts. Raiders kicker Errol Mann tied the game with a late field goal. It went into overtime. Neither team scored. So the game went into a second overtime. Stabler hit tight end Dave Casper for the winning score. Oakland won, 37–31. In the conference championship game, the Raiders met the Denver Broncos. Three turnovers led to Oakland's 20–17 loss.

RAIDERS
87

The Raiders went 9–7 in each of the next two seasons. They missed the playoffs. But what a decade it had been! The Raiders had won the AFC West six times. They made the playoffs seven times. They won their first Super Bowl. Oakland also earned a lasting reputation. It showed that it was willing to sign troublemakers, outcasts, and aging stars. Then it molded the players into a winning team.

QUARTERBACK JIM PLUNKETT

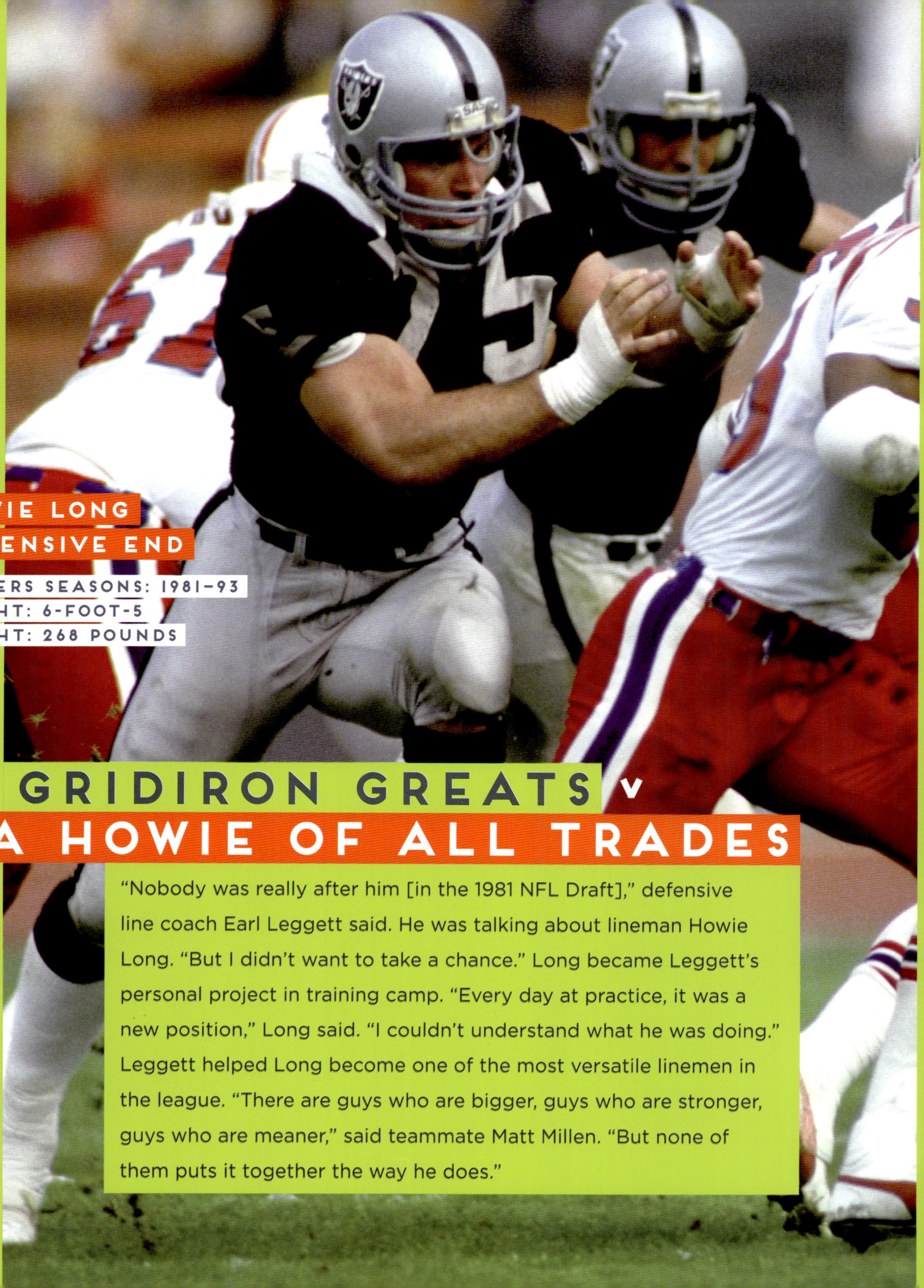

HOWIE LONG
DEFENSIVE END

RAIDERS SEASONS: 1981–93
HEIGHT: 6-FOOT-5
WEIGHT: 268 POUNDS

GRIDIRON GREATS

A HOWIE OF ALL TRADES

"Nobody was really after him [in the 1981 NFL Draft]," defensive line coach Earl Leggett said. He was talking about lineman Howie Long. "But I didn't want to take a chance." Long became Leggett's personal project in training camp. "Every day at practice, it was a new position," Long said. "I couldn't understand what he was doing." Leggett helped Long become one of the most versatile linemen in the league. "There are guys who are bigger, guys who are stronger, guys who are meaner," said teammate Matt Millen. "But none of them puts it together the way he does."

84

84 CAREER SACKS

179

179 GAMES PLAYED

TED HENDRICKS AND LESTER HAYES

Oakland went 11–5 in 1980. Two key players were cornerback Lester Hayes and quarterback Jim Plunkett. Hayes picked off an incredible 13 passes during the regular season. He nabbed five more in the playoffs. He earned Defensive Player of the Year honors. Plunkett was a veteran backup. He joined the Raiders in 1979 at the age of 32. He seemed to be near the end of his NFL career. But in 1980, Oakland lost three of its first five games. Plunkett came off the bench. He guided the Raiders to 9 wins in their next 11 games. Then they won three playoff games. Oakland became the first Wild Card team to reach the Super Bowl. It would face the Philadelphia Eagles. Few experts gave the Raiders a chance. But Plunkett capped the Raiders' incredible comeback. He launched an 80-yard touchdown pass to fullback Kenny King in the first quarter of the game. It was the longest in Super Bowl history. Plunkett passed for 261 yards. He added two more touchdown passes. Oakland won, 27–10. Plunkett was named the game's Most Valuable Player (MVP).

RAIDERS

MARCUS ALLEN

TO L.A. AND BACK AGAIN

In 1981, Oakland fell to 7–9. Then, Davis moved the Raiders to Los Angeles. He wanted to take advantage of the franchise's popularity in the larger Southern California market. The Raiders picked local hero Marcus Allen in the 1982 NFL Draft. The running back had just won the Heisman Trophy as college football's best player. In his rookie season, Allen rushed for 697 yards. He caught passes for 401 more. He scored 14 touchdowns. He was named Offensive Rookie of the Year. The defense got a makeover. Second-year defenseman Howie Long forced his way into the

LEFT: LYLE ALZADO

starting lineup. Oakland also signed defensive end Lyle "Darth Raider" Alzado. The rugged defense quickly won over L.A. fans.

In 1983, the Raiders went 12–4. They returned to the Super Bowl. Allen turned it into his own personal showcase. He rushed for 191 yards and two touchdowns. One touchdown came from a 74-yard run. The Raiders trounced the Washington Redskins, 38–9. It was Oakland's third Super Bowl title. "This has to be the greatest feeling of my life," Allen said. "I've been to the Rose Bowl. I've won the Heisman Trophy. But nothing is sweeter than this."

The Raiders compiled winning records in the next two seasons. But they were quickly bounced out of the playoffs each time. In 1987, another Heisman Trophy winner arrived. Running back Bo Jackson had a rare combination of speed and strength. He also played Major League Baseball. Jackson and Allen gave Los Angeles a potent one-two punch at running back. The Raiders found even more excitement the following year. The team drafted wide receiver Tim Brown. He was a dangerous weapon as a kick returner. Jackson and Brown racked up impressive statistics. Still, wins were in short supply.

Things picked up in 1990 when the Raiders went 12–4. Unfortunately, Jackson's bright career ended suddenly. He injured his hip in a playoff win against the Cincinnati Bengals. The next week, the Buffalo Bills trounced the

Raiders, 51–3, in the AFC championship. Success was hard to come by during the next few years. The Raiders either missed the playoffs entirely or lost in early rounds.

Davis moved the Raiders back to Oakland in 1995. Fans there were thrilled. The team went just 8–8 that season. Still, "The Black Hole" (Oakland Coliseum's seating section for the most enthusiastic fans) was a rowdy place once again.

BO JACKSON

GRIDIRON GREATS

MR. RAIDER

"Touchdown Timmy" Brown made an instant impact as a rookie. He led the league in kickoff returns. Combining those yards with his punt return, receiving, and rushing gains, Brown amassed a total of 2,317 yards. It was an NFL rookie record. He gave himself the nickname, "Mr. Raider." He lived up to it. Brown holds most of the team's receiving records. He played 240 games in 16 seasons with the Raiders. "We call him 'The Natural,'" coach Jon Gruden said. "You tell him one time, you show him one time, and you can expect perfection."

TIM BROWN

WIDE RECEIVER

RAIDERS SEASONS: 1988–2003

HEIGHT: 6 FEET

WEIGHT: 195 POUNDS

RAIDERS
CHARGERS

DEFENSEMEN TYVON BRANCH, DESMOND BRYANT, AND TOMMY KELLY

TRYING TO RIGHT THE SHIP

Once again, wins often proved elusive. During the next five seasons, Oakland failed to achieve a winning record. The Raiders jumped back to 12–4 in 2000. They shut out the Miami Dolphins in the divisional playoffs. But the Baltimore Ravens beat the Raiders in the next round. The following year, Oakland went 10–6. It battled New England in a snowy playoff game. The Patriots won in overtime, 16–13.

The Raiders stormed back in 2002. They finished 11–5. Veteran quarterback Rich Gannon had the best season of his career. He passed for 4,689 yards and 26 touchdowns. He won the league MVP award. It came in the 15th season of his career. The Raiders raced through two playoff games. They reached the Super Bowl for the first time in 19 years. There, they faced the Tampa Bay Buccaneers. Tampa Bay returned two interceptions for touchdowns. It demolished Oakland, 48–21.

After that, the Raiders went into a tailspin. They suffered losing records for the next seven seasons. Along the way, they claimed an undesirable title as the most penalized team in the NFL. The 2010 Raiders returned to modest respectability with an 8–8 record. The following season, Oakland had the chance to return to the playoffs. It needed to beat the San Diego Chargers in the season's final game. But it gave up 38 points in a disappointing loss. The team dropped to 4–12 in 2012 and 2013. It won just three games in 2014. The Raiders improved to 7–9 the following season.

In 2016, seven Pro Bowlers boosted the franchise. One was third-year quarterback Derek Carr. He led the Raiders to 12–4. It was their first winning record and playoff appearance in 14 seasons. But Carr broke his leg near the end of the regular season. As a result, Connor Cook became the first rookie quarterback to make his first start in a playoff game. He threw three interceptions. The Raiders lost to the Houston Texans, 27–14.

Big news was announced before the start of the 2017 season. The NFL approved the Raiders' relocation to Las

TACKLE ROBERT GALLERY

RUNNING BACK
DARREN MCFADDEN

CORNERBACK GAREON CONLEY

Vegas, Nevada. They would begin playing there in 2020. "We can turn the Silver State [Nevada's nickname] into the silver and black state," said team owner Mark Davis. On the field, the team lost its final four regular-season games to finish 6–10. In 2018, the Raiders dropped even lower, to 4–12.

The Raiders have experienced alternating eras of domination and futility. Author Mark Ribowsky once wrote that the team was a group of "odds and ends, oddities and irregulars, factory seconds and seeming chain-gang escapees." Players and fans alike are proud of their offbeat reputation. They wear it as a badge of honor as they chase their next Super Bowl title.

TEAM STATS

NFL CHAMPIONSHIPS

1976, 1980, 1983

WEBSITES

RAIDERS

https://www.raiders.com/

NFL: RAIDERS TEAM PAGE

http://www.nfl.com/teams/oaklandraiders/profile?team=OAK

INDEX

SAFETY TYVON BRANCH